CLASSIC BIRTHDAYS OF 20TH CENTURY POPULAR CULTURE CREATORS JULY AUGUST SEPTEMBER

....

A MEMORY CARE BOOK FOR ACTIVITY DIRECTORS AND CAREGIVERS

DAPHNE SIMPKINS

Copyright © 2025 Daphne Simpkins

All rights reserved. No part of this publication may be reproduced, distributed or transmitted in any form or by any means, including photocopying, recording, or other electronic or mechanical methods, without the prior written permission of the publisher, except in the case of brief quotations embodied in critical reviews and certain other noncommercial uses permitted by copyright law. For permission requests, write to the publisher at the email address below.

Daphne Simpkins/Quotidian Books
Contact: QuotidianToday@gmail.com

Classic Birthdays of 20th Century Popular Culture Creators July Aug Sept/Daphne Simpkins
ISBN 978-1-957435-21-3

Contents

Coming of Age on Memory Lane 9
Fireworks in July 13
July Classic Birthdays 16
Leslie Caron   July 1, 1931 17
Thomas A. Dorsey   July 1, 1899-January 23, 1993 20
Eva Marie Saint   July 4, 1924- 24
Janet Leigh   July 6, 1927-October 3, 2004 27
Oscar Hammerstein II   July 12, 1895-August 23, 1960 30
Ginger Rogers   July 16, 1911- April 25, 1995 34
Barbara Stanwyck   July 16, 1907-January 20, 1990 37
Erle Stanley Gardner   July 17, 1889 - March 11, 1970 40
Natalie Wood   July 20, 1938- Nov 29, 1981 43
John D. MacDonald   July 24, 1916-- Dec 28, 1986 47
Henry Ford   July 30, 1863-April 7, 1947 50
France Nuyen   July 31, 1939-- 55
August Classic Birthdays 57
Introduction to August 58
Myrna Loy   August 2, 1905-Dec 14, 1993 62
Louis Armstrong   August 4, 1901-July 6, 1971 65
Robert Mitchum   August 6, 1917-July 1, 1997 69
Lucille Ball   August 6, 1911-April 26, 1989 72
Norma Shearer   Aug 10, 1902-- June 12, 1983 76
Alfred Hitchcock   Aug 13, 1899 --April 9, 1980 80
Mae West   Aug 17, 1893-Nov 22, 1980 84
Gene Kelly   August 23, 1912-Feb 2, 1996 87
Lloyd C. Douglas   August 27, 1877-Feb 13, 1951 90

Ingrid Bergman Aug 29, 1915-Aug 29, 1982 93
Alan Jay lerner August 31, 1918- June 14, 1986 96
September Classic birthdays 99
Welcome to September 100
Edgar Rice Burroughs Sept 1, 1875-Mar 19, 1950 102
Bob Newhart September 5, 1929-July 18, 2024 105
Maurice Chevalier Sept 12, 1888-Jan 1, 1972 108
Claudette Colbert Sept 13, 1903-July 30, 1996 111
Agatha Christie Sept 15, 1890—Jan 12, 1976 114
Lauren Bacall Sept 16, 1924-Aug 12, 2014 118
George Gershwin Sept 26, 1898—July 11, 1937 122
Catherine Marshall Sept 27, 1914-March 18-1983 126
Ed Sullivan Sept 28, 1901-Oct 13, 1974 129
Greer Garson Sept 29, 1904—April 6, 1996 132
Gene Autry Sept 29, 1907-October 2, 1998 135
Johnny Mathis September 30, 1935— 140
Deborah Kerr Sept 30, 1921-Oct 16, 2007 143
Excerpt from BLESSED:Stories Confessions of a Recovering Caregiver
.... 146
Books by Daphne Simpkins 151

*For Activity Directors and Caregivers
who help to create special events and programs
For the people in their care*

"Anyone who stops learning is old, at twenty or eighty. Anyone who keeps learning stays young. The greatest thing in life is to keep your mind young."

–Henry Ford

COMING OF AGE ON MEMORY LANE

We all grow up and have coming-of-age moments.

It doesn't matter when you were born or what age you are now.

You have in common with other people of any age the event of change that is associated with a growth in understanding, maturity, and becoming who you are.

Sometimes these moments of change are referred to as epiphanic turning points. *We used to be like this, and now we are like this.*

It's not the particulars of the experience that make this kind of moment a universal experience; it is the event itself.

Different fields of study approach this event of change and assign agendas and name expectations of what could happen next.

Psychologists plumb the depths of coming-of-age moments to prompt self-revelation or bring consolation to an event that was painful, possibly traumatic.

Employers evaluate and hire candidates based on their resumes' timelines of career growth and the advancement of expertise.

Religious people might point to an event in their spiritual maturity and name that moment of change metanoia.

All these responses point to a truth about it, but only the person living the moment and reliving it later re-experiences the vitality stored in a memory that promoted personal change or growth.

That phrase "in the moment" feels awfully insignificant because it is so transitory. While the effect of remembering an episodic memory may only last a brief time, it has a potent, refreshing effect.

If someone is residing in an assisted living establishment or anywhere which is not their preferred homeplace, that touching time in a memory that makes you feel stronger is priceless.

If that person not only lives in an assisted living home and also in a body that manages chronic illness, the effect is even more profound.

Imagine feeling more at home in a place and your body by simply getting in touch with an episodic memory that resurrects essential personhood not defined by age or gender but by experience. We call that experience of the essential self "you-ness."

That experience of revitalizing you-ness happens more frequently when the activities scheduled for residents of assisted living homes tie into the cultural times of their growing up.

If you are half the age of the people in your assisted living home, how do you know who the people were your people know, the songs they sang or hummed or whistled, or the movies and books that created an emotional landscape that is linked to their emotional moments of you-ness?

This series of Memory Care books is intended to introduce Activity Directors and at-home caregivers to the popular culture touchstones that could prompt you-ness memories.

It is laid out in birthdays of 20th century popular culture creators because, most likely, an Activity Director or a caregiver knows and celebrates the birthdays of his/her residents. Weave the dates of popular culture creators into your in-house calendar of birthdays and you initiate the potent process of prompting an association with an artifact of time that could promote well-being. Well-being at any age is priceless.

FIREWORKS IN JULY

Maybe you will enjoy fireworks on the 4th of July. You light up the sky. You might hear firecrackers— wave sparklers.

But in the production and direction of movies while censorship was still guiding some of the dialogues and scenes, fireworks often served as a metaphor for passion. Hitchcock uses fireworks in the movie *To Catch a Thief* when Cary Grant and Grace Kelly flirt with one another in a way that can set off the kind of passionate exchange that wasn't allowed on screen, so you kind of let it happen in a night sky with shooting sparks.

In the early to mid-20th century, metaphors helped to tell the story on screen in the same way that the soundtrack of music that was developing as part of the movie itself steered emotions and emphasized tensions.

Creators of drama and forms of entertainment used what they knew of the senses to attract and engage viewers and readers—and there were devoted readers. Some serious readers belonged to direct mail book clubs which sent them hard copies of books each month with their subscription to the service. Dedicated readers often had library cards too and used them.

Back in the day, you could reserve a newly released book for ten cents that paid for the postcard which the librarian mailed you to let you know that the book you were dying to read was back in the library, and that it was your turn to check it out.

Those books could be by any author, but you would find eager readers for the latest John D. MacDonald, who wrote the Travis McGee books or the newest Erle Stanley Gardner, who wrote the Perry Mason series.

July is a month for fireworks (and metaphors) and reading because it is part of the summer vacation for students and parents. But it is also a month for traveling, which we often do in cars. Their popularity was launched by Henry Ford (in part) and his Model-T automobile, which you could have "in any color you liked as long as it was black."

The popular culture creators of July offer a lot of sizzle and none more than the first up Leslie Caron, who danced with Fred Astaire in *Daddy Long Legs* to the song *Something's Gotta Give.*

That kind of tension was represented by fireworks—and dance once upon a time. Meet some of the people who lived it.

JULY CLASSIC BIRTHDAYS

Leslie Caron July 1

Thomas A. Dorsey July 1

Eva Marie Saint July 4

Janet Leigh July 6

Oscar Hammerstein II July 12

Ginger Rogers July 16

Barbara Stanwyck July 16

Erle Stanley Gardner July 17

Natalie Wood July 20

John D. MacDonald July 24

Henry Ford July 30

France Nuyen July 31

LESLIE CARON
JULY 1, 1931

Actress and dancer Leslie Caron got her start in *An American in Paris*. Discovered and nurtured by the star Gene Kelly, Leslie Caron was surprised that dancers were called hoofers in America, and she regretted that word. It was coarse, not doing justice to the grace and beauty of dancing.

Leslie went on to showcase her lithe dancing ability in movies like *Daddy Long Legs*, but she did not star as a dancer in the tear-jerker movie *Fanny,* where she is portrayed as a young woman who is pregnant out of wedlock and cannot marry the man she loves. Instead, she marries another good and older man who proposes and provides for her and the baby. *Fanny* (1961) is a good movie with a lovely theme song.

In real life, opportunities increased for Caron, and later in her career, she starred in several episodes of the night-time soap opera *Falcon Crest* and also an episode of *Law and Order SVU*, for which she won an Emmy.

A versatile and wondrous entertainer, Leslie Caron tells her own story in the autobiography *Thank Heaven: A Memoir*. The title is allusion to a song that Maurice Chevalier sings in the movie *Gigi* (*Thank Heaven for Little Girls)*. Leslie plays Gigi.

Caron says of living in America: "The American is wholeheartedly for love and romance at any cost."

In 2008, Leslie became an American citizen just in time to vote for the first time in the presidential election.

About her desire to keep working, she said: "I think it's the end of progress if you stand still and think of what you've done in the past. I keep on."

Favorite movies showcasing the talents of Leslie Caron:
Fanny
Gigi
Daddy Long Legs
An American in Paris
Father Goose
Lili

Book: *Thank Heaven: A Memoir* by Leslie Caron.

THOMAS A. DORSEY
JULY 1, 1899-JANUARY 23, 1993

According to one biographer, Thomas A. Dorsey wrote music that "combined the good news of the gospel with the bad news of the blues."

In his day and in the days of W. C. Handy and Mahalia Jackson, there was tension between the right and wrong kind of music, the good and bad kind of music in church. The blues was often at odds with what were considered proper church hymns.

After his own personal and he believed "inspired" revelation of how to use his musical gifts, Dorsey went from being a blues player to a shaper of gospel music and to some he is called the Father of Gospel in the same way that W. C. Handy is known as the Father of the Blues.

Both men had spiritual backgrounds and training. Handy heard music in the world around him and composed the blues, primarily. Dorsey heard the good news of the gospel around him and wrote music that prompted more physical participation in the congregational singing in churches that included clapping and stomping.

Getting rowdy and loud in church was considered unrefined by traditionalists. Dorsey thought differently and stayed true to his vision of gospel music in the same way that Handy followed his of the blues.

Dorsey wrote over 3,000 songs and founded an organization to help train other church musicians and choirs: National Convention of Gospel Choirs and Choruses.

His work was so popular that when someone wanted a certain type of gospel song, they said, "Get me a Dorsey."

His success in life was not previewed by his humble origins. The son of Georgia sharecroppers, Dorsey struggled academically and dropped out of school after 4th grade. He befriended musicians and learned to play and write music informally with them.

And, in time, he married his first wife Nettie. She died giving birth to their son who also died shortly afterwards. That is when Dorsey wrote his most famous gospel song: *Take My Hand, Precious Lord.*

He continued to do his work, going from church to church teaching others how to sing for the glory of the Lord. His second wife Kathryn said of her busy, hard-working husband, "He was dedicated to saving souls through his songs."

Of his own work, Dorsey said, "I sat down at the piano and my hands began to browse over the keys. Then something happened. I felt as though I could reach out and touch God. I found myself playing a melody, one I'd never heard or played before, and words came into my head—they just seemed to fall into place."

Dorsey's extensive body of work includes:

Take My Hand, Precious Lord
There'll Be Peace in the Valley for Me
Old Ship of Zion
Hide Me in Thy Bosom
It's a Highway to Heaven
What Could I do If It Wasn't For the Lord
Search Me Lord
If You See My Savior

Mr. Dorsey died of Alzheimer's disease in 1993 at the age of 93.

EVA MARIE SAINT
JULY 4, 1924-

Married for 65 years to her husband Jeffrey Hayden (he died at the age of 90), Eva Marie Saint kick started her career opposite Marlon Brando in the classic movie *On the Waterfront.* She won the Oscar for Best Supporting Actress.

Soon after, Alfred Hitchcock placed Eva opposite Cary Grant in *North by Northwest*.

Then, the cool blonde co-starred with Paul Newman in *Exodus*, a movie about the formation of the state of Israel based upon the book by popular writer Leon Uris.

The mother of two and a devoted wife, Eva chose projects carefully but generally received positive reviews for her sensitivity and presence on the screen.

As popular as she was, Eva had other plans for her life. She was a wife and a mother and devoted to her family.

She had an agent once who wanted her to make more movies than she was already making. She told him, "I can't. I can only do one a year, if that. I have children, young children.' And he said, 'Well, I guess you won't be a superstar.' She replied, 'Well, I guess not.'

Eva Marie Saint became one anyway.

She had goals. She worked hard. She was good at her job! After her ninetieth birthday, Eva Marie Saint said: "You reach a certain age, and you're so proud that you're walking and breathing and loving and working and all of that at 90."

"The longer you live, the smarter you get because you've been around. You've seen things. You've gone through different emotional experiences in your own life, and hopefully, you understand things better. And that makes you a better actress."

When asked about age, she said: "You know how to stay young? Go with the flow."

The attitude has worked for her. She has been working in television and film. She is 100 years old and still smiling.

Favorite films featuring Eva Marie Saint:
North by Northwest
On the Waterfront
36 Hours
Nothing in Common
Gran Prix
Raintree County
The Sandpiper

JANET LEIGH
JULY 6, 1927-OCTOBER 3, 2004

Actress Norma Shearer saw a picture of Janet Leigh while on vacation and took it back to her husband Irving Thalberg, who managed the movie studio MGM.

Shearer explained, "That smile made it the most fascinating face I'd seen in years. I felt I had to show that face to somebody at the studio."

Her husband and the Studio Somebodies liked Janet's smile, too, and recruited the fledgling actress for *The Romance of Rosy Ridge.*

The audience loved her instantly. So did Alfred Hitchcock, who hired Janet Leigh for the shocking thriller *Psycho.*

Leigh said later that Hitchcock relished "scaring her" and that he used the prop of a dead woman's corpse to test Leigh's fearful response and in doing that tried to assess how an audience would feel about that same prop/corpse.

There was another twist to her performance as Marion Crane in *Psycho.* She dies, and usually main characters did not die in movies.

By all accounts, Leigh loved working with Hitchcock. However, she made many other marvelous movies with different directors that people enjoy today, including *Little Women, Touch of Evil,* and the Christmas classic *Holiday Affair.*

Janet is also famous for being married briefly to fellow actor Tony Curtis. The couple had a child that 21st century audiences recognize as the immensely popular Jamie Leigh Curtis.

After her divorce from Curtis, Janet married Robert Brandt.

Classic Birthdays of Popular Culture Creators of the 20th Century

They were together for 42 years until her death at the age of 77 from vasculitis.

Enjoyable movies with Janet Leigh:

Psycho
Bye Bye Birdie
The Romance of Rosie Ridge
The Manchurian Candidate
Holiday Affair
Wives and Lovers
Harper
Touch of Evil
Little Women

OSCAR HAMMERSTEIN II
JULY 12, 1895-AUGUST 23, 1960

Because movies made of his and Richard Rodgers musicals often integrate sentimentalism and romance, fans of Oscar Hammerstein II don't often realize that this Harlem-born lyricist and musical book writer was driven by a fierce sense of social justice.

You can hear it in songs like *You've Got to Carefully Taught* from the movie *South Pacific*, but the musicals themselves are also a form of promoting social change.

Hammerstein's impact on the 20th century began with his collaboration with Jerome Kern and their production of *Show Boat*, a musical inspired by popular writer Edna Ferber's book by the same name.

Other opportunities opened up for Hammerstein after that.

When Lorenz Hart backed out of writing with Richard Rodgers what would become *Oklahoma!*, Oscar said yes to replacing Hart. A powerful new partnership was formed that produced not only the transformation of the musical genre but would continue to produce shows that launched new voices in the theatre and explored themes that were true to life, such as:

The Nazi's oppression is experienced in *The Sound of Music*.

Domestic violence is revealed in *Carousel*.

Asian culture is introduced gently in *Flower Drum Song*.

Ethnic prejudice is laid bare in *South Pacific*.

The realms of power are also tested in *The King and I*.

Nominated many times by the Academy Awards (Oscars) for Best Song, Hammerstein and his collaborators won twice for *The Last Time I Saw Paris* and It Might as Well Be Spring.

Listen sometime to that latter song from *State Fair*. How does Oscar Hammerstein understand the moods of a young woman? He does, though. And the song deserved that award.

Known for pithy one-liners and quotable quotes, Hammerstein wrote this for the song *Happy Talk* in *South Pacific:* "You gotta have a dream. If you don't have a dream, how you gonna have a dream come true?"

The mentor of Stephen Sondheim, Oscar Hammerstein's last song was *Edelweiss* for the musical *The Sound of Music*, which became a movie after his death from stomach cancer at the age of 65.

Recommended biography of Oscar Hammerstein II: *Getting to Know Him: A Biography of Oscar Hammerstein II* by Hugh Fordin

Classic Birthdays of Popular Culture Creators of the 20th Century

Hammerstein's contributions to major musicals include:

The Sound of Music
The King and I
Oklahoma!
Carousel
Flower Drum Song
Show Boat
State Fair

GINGER ROGERS
JULY 16, 1911- APRIL 25, 1995

While some people think that Ginger Rogers's successful career in movies and musicals began with her mother's own ambitions for her daughter and her fascination with Hollywood, it was a actually a Charleston dance contest that launched Ginger's career in the performing arts.

Ginger danced the Charleston and won that competition; the prize was a six-month tour on the vaudeville circuit.

That success led to greater glory.

Over time she made nine films with co-star Fred Astaire. The pair and their musical movies made dancing while falling in love and singing love songs popular. The dancing duo launched some of the standards in music of what is now thought of as The Great American Songbook from the Golden Age of Hollywood.

But Ginger Rogers could do more than dance backwards while wearing high heels.

She was a beautifully nuanced dramatic actress who won the Oscar for her performance in *Kitty Foyle* and more admirers in the dramatic films: *I'll Be Seeing You* and *Tight Spot.*

Of her career, Ginger said: "The most important thing in anyone's life is to be giving something. The quality I can give is fun and joy and happiness. This is my gift."

About her working relationship with Fred Astaire, she said: "We had fun, and it shows."

A competitive tennis player, Rogers retired from acting in the 60s. She died of a heart attack at the age of 83.

DAPHNE SIMPKINS

Movies:

Kitty Foyle
Tight Spot
I'll Be Seeing You
Stage Door
Swing Time
Top Hat
The Barkleys of Broadway
Shall We Dance
Flying Down to Rio
Storm Warning
The Gay Divorcee
Carefree
Book: *Ginger: My Story* by Ginger Rogers

BARBARA STANWYCK
JULY 16, 1907-JANUARY 20, 1990

An observer of Barbara Stanwyck's life once said about the talented actress: "Barbara only lives for two things, and both of them are work."

Born Ruby Catherine Stevens, young Ruby was orphaned at an early age and sent to foster homes. She regularly ran away and never graduated from high school.

By age 14 Ruby was self-supporting and trying to break into show business. The break came, and because of her believable acting, she kept working and grew up with the motion picture industry.

She also changed her name to Barbara Stanwyck. Some of her greater successes include the dark drama *Double Indemnity*. But she made lasting impressions (though didn't win Oscars) for other classic movies, including *Stella Dallas*, *So Big*, *Christmas in Connecticut*, and *Sorry, Wrong Number*. She received an Honorary Oscar in 1982 for her life's work.

As her career in movies waned, Barbara moved into television work and starred in the western *The Big Valley (won an Emmy)* and, later, *The Thorn Birds (won an Emmy)*.

When not acting, she was involved in charity work.

Of her career, the actor said: "Just be truthful—and if you can fake that, you've got it made."

Married and divorced twice, Stanwyck was unmarried when she died of complications from COPD at the age of 82.

Classic Birthdays of Popular Culture Creators of the 20th Century

Her ashes were strewn over an area of land where she had made western movies.

Movies:
Stella Dallas
Christmas in Connecticut
Sorry, Wrong Number
Double Indemnity
Ball of Fire
Lady Eve
Titanic
Baby Face
Meet John Doe
Clash By Night
There's Always Tomorrow
Remember the Night
Executive Suite
East Side West Side
Golden Boy
My Reputation

ERLE STANLEY GARDNER
JULY 17, 1889 - MARCH 11, 1970

Raymond Burr as the living embodiment of Erle Stanley Gardner's famous fictional lawyer Perry Mason

When someone asked writer Erle Stanley Gardner why someone being shot by a handgun didn't die until the last bullet in the gun was fired, he replied, "I was paid by the word. Three cents a word. Bang. Bang. Bang. Bang. Bang. Bang."

Cha-ching.

That's one of the reasons the murder victims in his Perry Mason novels didn't die when the first shot was fired—or the second. The author wasn't just building suspense; he was making money by the word.

Mr. Gardner was trying to earn a living, writing as fast as he could, churning out what was called by some pulp fiction.

That kind of literature was for the avid reader who needed entertainment. That appetite still exists, but there are so many ways to meet it that the kind of books and short stories being written during Gardner's day have been replaced, in part, by television shows, blogs, and self-published books by prolific storytellers.

Automatically when you think of Perry Mason you might envision Raymond Burr (see above picture), but Burr tried out for the part of the prosecutor in the Perry Mason series initially. Devotees of the show know the name of Perry Mason's nemesis, the prosecutor Hamilton Burger.

But when Mr. Gardner saw Raymond Burr, he said, "He's the living embodiment of Perry Mason."

Almost as famous as the character is the theme song that introduced the show. While many call it the *Perry Mason* theme, its official title is *Park Avenue Beat* and it was composed by Fred Steiner, who wrote other well-received music for other popular televisions show in the 20th century, including *Twilight Zone, Rawhide, Gunsmoke,* and the original *Star Trek* television series.

After writing close to a hundred fifty novels which were published worldwide, Erle Stanley Gardner died of stomach cancer at the age of 80.

Popular novels by Gardner:
The Case of the Curious Bride
The Case of the Sleepwalker's Niece
The Case of the Substitute Face
The Case of the Shoplifter's Shoe
The Case of the Buried Clock

NATALIE WOOD
JULY 20, 1938- NOV 29, 1981

If you are a fan of the old movie *Miracle on 34th Street* (1947), you saw a very young Natalie Wood play a cynical child who is converted to the spirit of Christmas by the story of a man who plays Santa Claus in the Macy's Day's parade and believes he is St. Nick, too.

It's a delightful story still.

But Natalie also plays a different kind of child in the movie *Tomorrow is Forever* with Orson Wells and Claudette Colbert. With those dark eyes and solemn bearing, she brings a strong presence for someone who is just seven years old to the screen.

And that presence grows up in front of fans who see her coming of age on the screen.

In *Splendor in the Grass* with Warren Beatty, she suffers for love the way young lovers often do.

In *Rebel Without a Cause*, she explores excitement and the struggle to fit in with the famous James Dean.

In real life Natalie fell in love with Hollywood newcomer Robert Wagner.

The two were a popular Hollywood couple but eventually divorced—then got back together and married again.

And Natalie, after playing a variety of roles in very watchable movies, died tragically on a boat—drowning in such a way that others would question whether it was an accident or not.

That question was asked and answered many times. And Robert Wagner went on to have a long and successful career and write a couple of books that tell more of that story, if you are interested.

But for those of us who simply enjoy the older movies and the actresses who brought them to life, Natalie Wood is a beautiful and luminous actress who died young at the age of 43.

Movies to enjoy featuring Natalie Wood

Miracle on 34th Street
Tomorrow is Forever
Penelope
Splendor in the Grass
Rebel without a Cause
Brainstorm
This Property Is Condemned
West Side Story
Sex and the Single Girl
All the Fine Young Cannibals
Gypsy
Love With the Proper Stranger

Books:

Pieces of My Heart: A Life by Robert J. Wagner

You Must Remember This: Life and Style in Hollywood's Golden Age by Robert J. Wagner

JOHN D. MACDONALD
JULY 24, 1916-- DEC 28, 1986

This is not the typewriter John D. MacDonald used, but it is an example of the kind of manual typewriter that helped him to create his body of fiction.

More famous than the author John D. MacDonald is the character he created that represented manhood and a different kind of detective in the 20th century: Travis McGee.

A free thinker with a best pal Meyer, who was a brainy economist, Travis lived on a houseboat called

The Busted Flush but solved crimes on land and sea. He was fearless and smart and funny—and ladies, of course, fell for him hard but often left him later. (His nomadic life style ultimately didn't always appeal to women who wanted to settle down with the man they loved, and a man who will settle down doesn't usually live on a houseboat).

Some of the themes that Travis investigates are timely still—the environment, retirement, justice for common people, and the effects of industrialized progress all get explored in this series of books created by a man whose biography is called: *The Red Hot Typewriter: The Life and Times* of John D. MacDonald by Hugh Merrill.

John D., as he is affectionately known by his fans, wrote other pulp fiction before he invented Travis, but he also wrote other major novels that appealed to a broad populace, including *Cape Fear,* which has twice been made into a movie. The first incarnation is with Gregory Peck and Robert Mitchum; the more recent version starred Robert de Niro and Nick Nolte.

John D. was supposed to grow up to become his father's idea of a proper businessman, but he became a writer instead. His stories added significantly to the American psyche and explored values associated with homelife, working for a living, and what justice looks like when the courts can't mete it out.

John D. wrote 21 novels featuring Travis McGee and scores of other very entertaining stories.

He passed away at the age of 70 from complications with heart surgery.

Top titles to enjoy written by John Dann MacDonald:

The Dreadful Lemon Sky
The Quick Red Fox
Nightmare in Pink
A Deadly Shade of Gold
Dress Her in Indigo
The Empty Copper Sea
A Purple Place for Dying

Book: *The Red Hot Typewriter: The Life and Times of John D. MacDonald* by Hugh Merrill

HENRY FORD
JULY 30, 1863-APRIL 7, 1947

When he was twelve years old, Henry Ford received a pocket watch. He promptly took it apart to see how it worked. Afterwards, he took apart other people's watches and became known as a watch repairman. Thus began the career trajectory of the man who would found the Ford Motor Company, advocate for a five-day work week, believe that the customer needed to be served above all else, and maintained against popular opinion that smoking was bad for you.

Success wasn't a straight line.

His father had other plans for his boy.

Ford declined to run the farm his father wanted him to manage. Instead, he pursued his interest in machines. He worked on steam engines for Westinghouse. But he thought steam was too dangerous for a car. After he saw his first motor, he built a car at his house. Then he built two more cars. He drove one a thousand miles to see if it would hold up.

That was the beginning of what would become his company and previewed other ways that he would transform the Industrial Revolution and the nature of family life in America.

Ford had ideas about success. He believed that obstacles were what you saw when you took your focus off your goal. He believed that service to the customer brought more profits. He also acted on the belief that failure just taught you how to start again more intelligently.

He began with his famous Model-T, and then he sowed seeds of building independent car dealer franchises in the country that others could run.

The benefit went to American families who were enabled to afford transportation that broadened their experience of their country and knowledge of their neighbors.

He was a good neighbor to others, and in 1916, he released a pamphlet warning the American public of the dangers of smoking cigarettes. Thomas Edison wrote a letter supporting Ford's view. At the time, the idea was controversial. The document is called *The Case Against the Little White Slaver*. (It's available to read for free or download from Google books.)

While Ford was changing the American landscape, his wealth grew. He became one of the richest men in the world. He had one son, Edsel who died of stomach cancer at the age of 49.

As his own health began to decline, Ford ceded his company to his grandson Henry Ford II in 1945.

He left his wealth to the Ford Foundation.

Of his life, Ford said: One of the greatest discoveries a man makes, one of the great surprises, is to find he can do what he was afraid he couldn't do."

He passed away at the age of 83 from a cerebral hemorrhage.

Books:

Henry Ford: My Life and Work by Henry Ford

Ford philosophies:

"Failure is simply the opportunity to begin again, this time more intelligently."

"If everyone is moving forward together, then success takes care of itself."

"Anyone who stops learning is old, whether at twenty or eighty. Anyone who keeps learning stays young. The greatest thing in life is to keep your mind young."

"There are no big problems, there are just a lot of little problems."

"I believe God is managing affairs and that He doesn't need any advice from me. With God in charge, I believe everything will work out for the best in the end. So, what is there to worry about."

FRANCE NUYEN
JULY 31, 1939--

A French-American actress, France Nuyen is best known for her role of Liat in the Rodgers and Hammerstein musical *South Pacific.* She was the love interest of a lieutenant and sang the song *Happy Talk* to him. He sang *Younger Than Springtime* to her.

But she is also remembered for launching on Broadway the play *The World of Suzie Wong,* which is the story of a young woman making her living working and dancing in bars most often with servicemen. (The movie was made later, but it starred Nancy Kwan and William Holden.)

Fans can also find France in a movie based upon a Pearl Buck story, *Satan Never Sleeps.* Her co-star is William Holden. Critics hated the movie.

Married and divorced twice, Nuyen began a second career as a psychological therapist after her work in acting waned.

When interviewed about her life, Nuyen replied cryptically with an old proverb: "I am Chinese. I am a stone. I go where I am kicked."

Nuyen was also able to find work in different television series, including *The Man from U.N.C.L.E, Gunsmoke, Star Trek, Hawaii Five-O, Charlie's Angels, Columbo,* and *I Spy,* where she met her second husband Robert Culp.

Enjoyable movies featuring France Nuyen:
Diamond Head
The Joy Luck Club
South Pacific

AUGUST CLASSIC BIRTHDAYS

Myrna Loy August 2
Louis Armstrong August 4
Robert Mitchum August 6
Lucille Ball August 6
Norma Shearer August 10
Alfred Hitchcock August 13
Mae West August 17
Gene Kelly August 23
Lloyd C. Douglas August 27
Ingrid Bergman August 29
Alan Jay Lerner August 31

INTRODUCTION TO AUGUST

"Drama is life with the dull bits left out," said famed director of suspense thrillers Alfred Hitchcock. We celebrate his birthday this month!

Hitchcock was also fascinated with motives for murder, tricks the mind and memory play on people, and how memory functions.

How the mind works both in characters on the screen and in the people who watched his movies were aspects of Hitchcock's storytelling skills, and in this way, most people share the same curiosity. We're always trying to figure out who other people are, who we are, and who we are with other people.

Memory plays a driving force in this sleuthing out of the human condition, for memory is a storehouse of knowledge. We move the pieces around to make sense of the world around us.

When that ability to access memories and push them around in a way that fits what we consider logic, other conclusions are drawn. Inferences, really. For access to memories and how we use them leads to many a conclusion of early dementia and not being able to relate to others increases experiences of isolation and loneliness. One of the reactions is to retreat inward, which doesn't help anyone thrive.

Retreating, being excluded, and misunderstood results in all kinds of ways that make people feel out of step with contemporary society.

To alleviate that strain simple moments of recognition ease the feelings of isolation and can cause you to remember not who other people are but who you are at your core, which always exists however your brain is working on the surface where communication happens.

One of the ways to woo people to that place of comfort is to provide opportunities to revisit and remember touchstones of common culture with familiar faces on screen.

We know drama on the screen.

But personal drama that builds us as individuals is referred to by some neuroscientists as episodic memories. (There are all kinds of memories.)

Episodic memories are deeply personal and intrinsically true to who people really are without the masks we wear publicly.

In cases where dementia has taken hold, those masks are mostly gone or slipping away, but the core identity of that person is still there. Building a memory bridge to cause someone to reach that interior episodic memory can result in a refreshing moment of strength: a memory of he or she is deeply inside.

Any memory prompt can trigger it.

Scary things can draw it out.

Calm things can bring it to life.

Music can energize it.

A familiar face can.

A funny scene can.

A reference to an old movie or character that no one mentions anymore because contemporary administrators sometimes don't know the shows and movies and music that were part of people growing up and coming of age.

These artists, actors, storytellers or musicians are often labeled as classic, but they, like the director Alfred Hitchcock, are no more classic than the birthdays of the people who are often dependent upon caregivers in professional or homeplace situations.

Classic Birthdays of Popular Culture Creators of the 20th Century

Famous or not famous, younger or older, we all share the universal experience called coming of age, and we never stop coming of age.

Welcome to August and the dramas its popular culture creators have helped to produce and the memories they have helped to make.

MYRNA LOY
AUGUST 2, 1905-DEC 14, 1993

After gangster John Dillinger was famously shot down at the theatre where Myrna Loy's newest movie *Manhattan Melodrama* with Clark Gable was running, her career got a big boost.

It was reported that Dillinger considered Myrna Loy his favorite actress, and people went to see the movie to find out what the famed gangster saw in her and what she was doing just before her biggest fan died.

Previously Myrna Loy's career had been on a kind of slow start. She began in silent movies, playing mostly exotic women who were often a vamp or some kind of femme fatale. As silent movies transformed into talkies, Myrna found a new on-screen presence in a series of detective stories called *The Thin Man*, where she co-starred with William Powell.

Six movies later, Myrna had left behind the exotic vamp image and become a steady-as-she-goes housewife in movies like *Mr. Blandings Builds His Dream House* and the truly classic wartime drama *The Best Years of Our Lives.*

But she also played women with problems, and you will see her struggling with motherhood and alcohol in the watchable soap opera film *From the Terrace*.

Married and divorced four times, Loy was committed to working with the American Red Cross. Later in her career, she appeared in some television programs and some productions in theatres on Broadway. Although she never won an Oscar from an individual performance, she was awarded an Oscar for her life's work in 1991.

After surviving treatment for breast cancer, her health began to fail. She died at the age of 88 from natural causes.

Marvelous movies with Myrna Loy:
The Thin Man Movies
Mr. Blandings Builds His Dream House
Cheaper By the Dozen
From the Terrace
Manhattan Melodrama
The Best Years of Our Lives

Her autobiography: *Being and Becoming: A Memoir* by Myrna Loy

LOUIS ARMSTRONG
AUGUST 4, 1901-JULY 6, 1971

"Every time I close my eyes blowing that trumpet of mine—I look right in the heart of good old New Orleans...It has given me something to live for."

It's amazing what Louis Armstrong remembers and saw in good old New Orleans because he grew up in one of the worst parts of it called The Battlefield. Poverty reigned there, and people struggled to make a living.

Born to a sixteen-year-old girl, Louis spent the first few years of his life with his grandmother before his mother could take him back. But even then, his young mama didn't raise him. Louis grew up on the streets, working alongside a Jewish family—the Karnofskys—who kept him fed and sheltered him and demonstrated the kind of kindship that people who grow up in poverty together share and don't forget.

One must wonder if when Louis blew his horn and looked into good old New Orleans he was thinking of the goodness of his neighbors. He wore a Star of David all of his life in kinship and memory of their helping him.

Louis needed help. He got into trouble with the law from a random act of using a weapon thoughtlessly, and while incarcerated he began to play the cornet. Later he would play the trumpet.

But it wasn't only his command of the instrument that earned him commercial success and the nickname Satchmo and as he aged, Pops. His upbeat personality and engaging smile and ability to josh with the audience made him immensely popular, earning him access to all levels of society.

None of that success went to his head. He was an entertainer who worked well with others but also developed his solo abilities. He also helped to create jazz: a genre of music that he smiled about when someone asked him to define it and said, "If you have to ask what jazz is you'll never know...."

And he made a few songs in the American Songbook famous for all time: *What a Wonderful World, Hello, Dolly, On the Sunny Side of the Street, Dream a Little Dream of Me*, and *La Vie En Rose*. He improvised sometimes. He helped invent a kind of syllable singing called scat, and he was good friends with other entertainers, like Bing Crosby, who admired him and was heavily influenced in his singing by Armstrong.

After some disappointing marriages, Louis married Lucille Wilson, a singer at the Cotton Club, and they remained married until his death.

He died at the age of 69 from a heart attack.

Bing Crosby said that Louis Armstrong was "the greatest singer than ever was and ever will be."

Signature songs: *What a Wonderful World, Stardust, Dream a Little Dream of Me, Hello, Dolly, Ain't Misbehavin', When the Saints Go Marchin' In*

You can enjoy seeing Louis Armstrong in these movies:

High Society
The Glenn Miller Story
Hello, Dolly!
Paris Blues
The Five Pennies
Cabin in the Sky
Pennies From Heaven

Books: *Satchmo: My Life in New Orleans* by Louis Armstrong

What Louis Armstrong said:

"I was born in what they call the poor man's Storyville. But it was always the Red-Light District, or just District to me. And will be in my memory the rest of my life."

"I think I had a beautiful life. I didn't wish for anything I couldn't get, and I got pretty near everything I wanted because I worked for it. I don't keep nothing I can't use right now, so everything I have I'm still enjoying it."

ROBERT MITCHUM
AUGUST 6, 1917-JULY 1, 1997

Although he played a wide range of characters, Robert Mitchum was truly menacing in *Cape Fear (1962)* written by John D. MacDonald.

But he had other facets to his onscreen persona.

Robert Mitchum was temptation for Deborah Kerr in *The Grass is Greener,* where, Kerr, temporarily dissatisfied with her daily married life with husband Cary Grant, drifts into a serious flirtation with Mitchum.

In another movie, playing a nun, Deborah respects Robert's robust physical strength as her protector in *Heaven Knows, Mr. Allison.*

Mitchum and Kerr teamed up again in the movie *The Sundowners*, a story about life in the Australian outback.

Kerr wasn't the only leading lady who enjoyed working with Robert Mitchum.

He flirted with Loretta Young in an under-appreciated black and white movie *Rachel and The Stranger.*

He continues to charm modern fans in the Christmas classic movie *Holiday Affair* where he falls hard for sweet Janet Leigh.

And Mitchum famously demonstrated onscreen chemistry with Jane Russell in *His Kind of Woman.*

About his acting, Mitchum joked, "Listen. I've got three expressions: looking left, looking right and looking straight ahead."

He was a better actor than his self-effacing description intimates. Nominated for an Oscar for his performance in *The Story of G. I. Joe,* Mitchum was routinely sought to star in war movies and westerns—in stories where the leading man was a manly man. He had a "rugged dignity."

They also called Mitchum a straight shooter.

Again, Mitchum said of how people see him: "People think I have an interesting walk. Hell, I'm just trying to hold my gut in."

Married to his wife Dorothy from 1940 until his death from emphysema in 1997, he said that he had met the best of women in his work but not a single one of them could hold a candle to his wife Dorothy.

Movies with Robert Mitchum:
Out of the Past
The Story of G. I. Joe
El Dorado
The Night of the Hunter
River of No Return
Heaven Knows, Mr. Allison
The Grass is Greener
Holiday Affair
Rachel and the Stranger
His Kind of Woman
Out of the Past
The Longest Day

LUCILLE BALL
AUGUST 6, 1911-APRIL 26, 1989

At the height of the popularity of the TV show *I Love Lucy,* Marshall Fields, a big department store, closed down early for the night.

The reason?

Very few customers shopped on the night that Lucy was on TV.

Marshall Fields posted a sign to explain why they weren't open to the few people who might trickle their way which read: **Closed. We love Lucy, too.**

That might have amused Lucy, but it most likely didn't surprise her. By multiple accounts, Lucille Ball was an incredibly shrewd businesswoman.

Successful, loved by all, hard-working Lucy made a surprising statement about her life. She said that success didn't begin for her until she had her first child at the age of 41. Lucy loved being a mother!

Fans may recall that she was pregnant on *I Love Lucy* and gave birth to Little Ricky. The shows about being pregnant were her favorite shows, Lucy recalled later.

Later was after she divorced Desi Arnez, the ex-husband she still loved and whom she described in retrospect as a great showman but also as a kind of Jekyll/Hyde fellow who drank too much, gambled too much, and fooled around with other women way too much.

Lucy was able to maintain her popularity after the divorce.

Lucy set a pattern for homemakers and dreamers and also established a pattern for making sitcoms, a new genre of television entertainment.

What was different about the *I Love Lucy* series, however, was that she and Desi captured the programs on film and retained copies, thinking later they could be a series of home movies they could enjoy in their old age.

What happened instead was that they built a fortune, for in the taping of the shows they invented what was to become the norm: the rerun.

Reruns make big money over time.

And they owned them.

It was only after the business became more than she wanted to manage that Lucy sold out the big Desilu operation and built something smaller to promote a series of subsequent sitcoms that never equaled her earlier success.

Neither did many of her movies, like *Mame.*

But that didn't deter the inveterate performer from working hard and loving her children, which is where her heart was located.

She also married again after the divorce from Desi, writing to a friend that "she had picked a winner" in

Gary Morton, a comedian and someone who took very good care of her.

When asked about her success, Lucy didn't claim comedic timing or great skill at dramatic acting. Instead, she gave the writers and her co-stars the credit for the writing and ideas. She said of herself: "What I am is brave."

That's something Lucy knew about herself and practiced until her passing at the age of 77 from an aortic aneurism. Her death made the front-page headlines of many national newspapers.

Her home movies, better known as the reruns of *I Love Lucy,* continue to entertain people day and night all over the world.

In addition to her classic sitcom I Love Lucy, Ms. Ball appeared in the following movies:

Stage Door
The Long, Long Trailer
Mame
Dubarry Was a Lady
Yours, Mine, and Ours

NORMA SHEARER
AUG 10, 1902-- JUNE 12, 1983

Norma Shearer's mother sold the family dog and the family piano to get enough money to move herself and her two daughters to Hollywood to try and break into the picture business.

It was a big gamble.

She was counting on Norma, who wasn't particularly pretty and had a cast in one eye that made her look cross-eyed in person and on the screen.

But Norma had goals, and she said later an "almost dangerous belief in herself."

The wanna-be actress learned some exercises that would help her eyes to look better on screen for a few hours, and she did the exercises faithfully.

She also learned how to stand in the right light to look better than she did in the wrong light.

And when person after person told her after a series of negative try-outs that she didn't have what it takes to succeed as an actress, Norma persevered because she was, in her own words, "ferociously ambitious."

That dangerous belief in herself and the permission she gave herself to be ambitious in a time when women were often thought of as unladylike when they were, gained Norma a contract with a movie studio after three years of hearing a lot of no's.

Living conditions had been poor until then, but they got better when Norman began to draw a $250 a week salary from the studio.

Over time, her acting skills improved, and she was ultimately nominated for six Best Actress Oscar awards, winning only for *The Divorcee.*

Seen as a strong woman on the screen (but differently than the way Bette Davis and Joan Crawford were cast as strong women too), Norma Shearer made it all right to be "single and not a virgin," wrote one commentator.

That strength helped her personally, too.

Norma forged strong friendships and married a powerful man in the picture business, Irving Thalberg. He managed the MGM movie studio.

They were a successful couple. Irving died in 1936 and left his estate to Norma. The studio resisted giving her what Irving had bequeathed to her. She fought a legal battle with MGM, and she won.

In 1942, Norma retired from acting, dated some, and finally married her second husband who was 11 years her junior. They were together until her death at the age of 80 from pneumonia.

Her best movies according to critics:
The Divorcee
The Barretts of Wimpole Street
The Women
Romeo and Juliet
A Free Soul
Marie Antoinette

Classic Birthdays of Popular Culture Creators of the 20th Century

Book: *Norma Shearer: A Biography* by Gavin Lambert

ALFRED HITCHCOCK
AUG 13, 1899 --APRIL 9, 1980

British-born movie director Alfred Hitchcock is most famous for scaring people who want to be scared.

Why some of us like to be scared and call that entertainment is something to think about later.

Hitchcock said of his motivation for making his kind of movies: "The only way to get rid of my fears is to make films about them."

The legendary director must have been afraid of heights because characters dangle dangerously in *North by Northwest, Rear Window,* and *Vertigo.*

Hitchcock must have also been afraid of nature turning against mankind too because that happens in *The Birds.*

He must have worried about the murderous, dark side of human nature as well because we experience that in *Rope, Shadow of a Doubt, Suspicion,* and *Dial M for Murder.*

And that's not all that Alfred Hitchcock produced.

In addition to his movies, considered classics, he moved into television and hosted a weekly drama. Hitchcock left his imprint there, too.

Famous in real life for having a rather course view of actors and for pushing actors outside of their comfort zones, Hitchcock produced movies that made people afraid to take a shower or go on a picnic if birds were overhead or gathering perched on children's playground equipment nearby.

Of his movies Hitchcock opined, "The length of a film should be directly related to the endurance of the human bladder."

Famous for preferring a cool blonde as his female lead instead of a brunette (although he makes an exception for *The Paradine Case)*, Hitchcock hired some of the most successful actors and actresses of the 20th century, often launching their careers.

However, some of the actresses thought he pushed them too far and in the case of Tippi Hedren who starred in *Marnie* and *The Birds,* she felt harassed by Hitchcock—miserably so.

While Hitchcock's nature in real life gets examined from many perspectives these days, his movies helped to create going to the cinema in the 20th century a special occasion; and when Hitchcock's movies rerun on late night classic channels or in honor of his or some actor's birthday, they are still enjoyable to watch.

Alfred Hitchcock passed away from natural causes with his wife of 54 years Alma at his side. He was 80 years old.

In addition to his body of work, Hitchcock left behind advice for future directors:

"The more successful the villain, the more successful the picture."

"There is no terror in the bang, only in the anticipation of it."

Favorite Alfred Hitchcock thrillers:

To Catch a Thief
Rear Window
Dial M for Murder
The Birds
Strangers on a Train
The Paradine Case
Suspicion
Shadow of a Doubt
Rope
Psycho
The Man Who Knew Too Much

Recommended biography: *The Dark Side of Genius: The Life of Alfred Hitchcock* by Donald Spoto

MAE WEST
AUG 17, 1893 - NOV 22, 1980

One of the major creators of entertainment in her time, the bawdy Mae West proclaimed with great zest, "Too much of a good thing can be wonderful."

Her one-line drawls were often laden with double-entendre, including the most famous, "Why don't you come on up and see me sometime?" She said about how others see her: "If I asked for a cup of coffee, someone would search for a double meaning."

West pushed boundaries on what was acceptable in bawdy entertainment and often faced legal consequences for her work. For her what was considered obscenity in her play *Sex*, written in 1936, Mae West spent 8 days in jail. (She was sentenced to ten days, but was released two days early for good behavior!)

Mae West was funny, original, likable, and easily quoted. "I believe in censorship. After all, I made a fortune out of it."

With mischief in her eyes and voice, Mae West teased, "Good girls go to heaven. Bad girls go everywhere else."

After a stroke, Mae West died at the age of 88. She said about living: "You only live once, but if you do it right, once is enough."

Movies: Legendary movies featuring the bawdy Mae West, include:

She Done Him Wrong
My Little Chickadee
Go West Young Man
Goin' To Town
I'm No Angel

Books:

Goodness Had Nothing to Do With It: The Autobiography of Mae West

GENE KELLY
AUGUST 23, 1912-FEB 2, 1996

Gene Kelly had some very decided views about the nature of dance and what dancing should look like on stage and in movies.

Unlike the sophisticated presence of esteemed dancer Fred Astaire, Gene Kelly believed that dancing for men could be athletic, and this athleticism included ballet.

In fact, Gene is credited with helping to make ballet socially acceptable for men.

Dancing athletically didn't go with a top hat and tails. Kelly believed his kind of dancing required a different taste in clothing—clothing that was also a costume in a performance.

He preferred his dance costume to be casual clothes and ordinary socks; and if a rain puddle got in your way, splash in it and sing a little. Kelly did just that in one of his most famous musicals, *Singin' in the Rain.*

But he was most successful in achieving his vision for dance and ballet in the classic musical *An American in Paris,* a storyline with music inspired by the last work of George Gershwin. You'll hear the song *Our Love Is Here to Stay* in that movie, and you will see the kind of dancing that Kelly believed should be included.

Just as the age of musicals was winding down, Kelly did what he could to preserve the art form by participating in *That's Entertainment!* and other films that tell the story of music and dance in America.

But he also took on dramatic roles, and you will see him raise a few surprised eyebrows by playing the part of a serious reporter in the classic drama *Inherit the Wind*.

Gene Kelly passed away at the age of 83 after suffering a series of strokes.

Movies with Gene Kelly:

Singin' in the Rain
An American in Paris
Inherit the Wind
Anchors Away
On the Town
Brigadoon
That's Entertainment!

LLOYD C. DOUGLAS
AUGUST 27, 1877-FEB 13, 1951

Image advertising the movie inspired by the book Magnificent Obsession by Lloyd C. Douglas

Lloyd C. Douglas was a late bloomer. The Protestant minister wrote his first novel when he was fifty, and *Magnificent Obsession* was an immediate success.

The storyline and theme lived up to the tradition of classic stories aligned wholesomely with the Bible.

But Douglas explored an unlikely theme. He explored the benefits of being generous anonymously.

That's quite a divergence in a capitalist society that presently touts its own generosity and has pictures made of oversized checks written to help people who are hungry or in need.

For Douglas, giving quietly with no one knowing what you were doing and taking no credit for what you gave or were giving, was the bigger adventure.

Readers and movie-goers agreed, making Lloyd C. Douglas one of the most successful writers of the 50s.

That first book *Magnificent Obsession* was made into a successful movie starring Jane Wyman and Rock Hudson. (See image above!)

Other movies made from Douglas's books did not always suit the writer, and he said so, attempting to add provisions or stipulations to filming other stories of his like *The Big Fisherman* and *The Robe*.

Douglas wrote his autobiography after stating that he was giving up fiction writing, but he only finished the first volume. He second volume was completed posthumously after his death by his two daughters.

Of his work, Douglas said: "There is no vanity so damaging to a man's character as pride over his good deeds!"

Douglas died of heart trouble at the age of 73.

Books:
Magnificent Obsession
The Robe
The Big Fisherman
Green Light
White Banners
Forgive Us Our Trespasses
Disputed Passage

Popular movies made from Douglas's books:
Magnificent Obsession
The Robe
The Big Fisherman
Green Light

INGRID BERGMAN
AUG 29, 1915-AUG 29, 1982

A kiss is just a kiss.

A sigh is just a sigh.

Those lyrics don't define Ingrid Bergman, but they often come to mind of fans of hers who still love the classic movie *Casablanca,* where she played opposite Humphrey Bogart.

Star-crossed lovers—split apart by a war and the resurfacing of her husband—Ingrid and Humphrey find each other again in a gin joint he owns, and there his piano player Sam resurrects the song of timeless love. *You must remember this. A kiss is just a kiss. A sigh is just a sigh.* The song is called *As Time Goes By.*

"I don't know why people like that movie," she said wonderingly. *Cascablanca* wasn't her personal favorite, though she is in the minority for her fans love it.

Ingrid preferred many of her other films like *Gaslight, Spellbound, Notorious, Saratoga Trunk, For Whom The Bell Tolls,* and *Indiscreet.*

The movie *Indiscreet* with Cary Grant poked fun in a gentle way at falling in love inconveniently (in public) with a man you cannot have or should not have. That happened to Ingrid when she fell in love with Roberto Rossellini while married to a husband who was more business manager than lover. She left her husband for Roberto. Scandal followed her. And that scandal dampened her career—for a while.

She returned as time went by and found a more forgiving audience and more mature roles.

One of her last movies was *The Yellow Rolls-Royce,* an entirely wonderful movie in which plays a valiant hero in the story.

She passed away from breast cancer at the age of 67.

Movies:
A Woman Called Golda
Murder on the Orient Express
Autumn Sonata
Indiscreet
Casablanca
For Whom the Bells Toll
Saratoga Trunk
Notorious
Spellbound
Gaslight

Interesting biography of Ingrid: *Notorious: The Life of Ingrid Bergman* by Donald Spoto

ALAN JAY LERNER
AUGUST 31, 1918- JUNE 14, 1986

In addition to being known as a great lyricist, Alan Jay Lerner could also be called The Marrying Man.

He married eight times. He wrote a lot of love songs to commemorate those special feelings, admitting that he liked the good times of falling in love but not the difficulties that happened later.

Perhaps the best known of his eight wives is the actress Nancy Olson (*Sunset Boulevard*), who didn't know that her first husband would go on to marry five more times after he left her for a high-strung woman in France. (Not much is known about Micheline except that she ran Alan a merry chase. You might discern some of his lament in the lyrics from *Camelot*, in a song called *How To Handle a Woman*).

Major musicals with seriously wonderful music include: *Gigi, Camelot, My Fair Lady, Brigadoon,* and *On A Clear Day You Can See Forever.*

The American Classic Songbook hosts many of the treasures co-written mostly with Frederick Loewe.

Favorite Lerner songs include:
If Ever I Would Leave You (the irony is not lost on any of his wives)
I Could Have Danced All Night
I've Grown Accustomed To Her Face
On the Street Where You Live

In his autobiography, *The Street Where I Live*, you will meet the affable man so many women found attractive. He credits his dad, also a philanderer, with cultivating his love of language. Whenever he wrote to his father, his dad would write notes in the margin suggesting ways his son could have expressed himself better.

Later in life and a patient of the infamous amphetamine pushing Dr. Feelgood, Lerner was addicted to the amphetamine shots that the concierge doctor administered. He passed away from lung cancer at the age of 67 without enough money to pay his own medical expenses. Most of his estate was tied up in paying off ex-wives.

Quote. "Why can't a woman be more like a man?"

Musical productions:

My Fair Lady
Camelot
Brigadoon
Paint Your Wagon
Gigi

Autobiography: *The Street Where I Live* by Alan Jay Lerner

SEPTEMBER CLASSIC BIRTHDAYS

Edgar Rice Burroughs   September 1

Bob Newhart September 5

Maurice Chevalier September 12

Claudette Colbert September 13

Agatha Christie September 15

Lauren Bacall September 16

George Gershwin September 26

Catherine Marshall September 27

Ed Sullivan September 28

Greer Garson September 29

Gene Autry September 29

Johnny Mathis September 30

Deborah Kerr September 30

WELCOME TO SEPTEMBER

This month hosts a variety of talented people from comedians to musicians.

Debonair and very French Maurice Chevalier sings about memory in the song *I Remember It Well*.

Composer George Gershwin promised *Our Love Is Here To Stay* and we hear Gene Kelly sing it *in An American in Paris*.

Singing Cowboy Gene Autry represented a mostly forgotten kind of music called The Horse Opera and is best remembered for making popular some choice Christmas songs like *Rudolph the Red-Nosed Reindeer* and *Frosty the Snowman*.

Johnny Mathis could sing anything well and did! Remember *A Certain Smile*? *The Twelfth of Never*? *Chances Are*?

And while Deborah Kerr ostensibly sang in both *The King and I* and *An Affair to Remember*, her voice was dubbed. You may never have heard of Marni

Nixon, but if you have seen those movies, you have heard her sing.

But we also have some writers this month who have left a legacy of good stories and some interesting questions. Agatha Christie is the Queen of Mystery Writing. Catherine Marshall celebrated the preaching skills of her late husband Peter and then wrote books that kept other widows and pilgrims company.

But before we get to all those birthdays, meet the first birthday boy of the month. His name is Edgar Rice Burroughs, and he invented one of the most popular characters to ever play on Saturday afternoons: Tarzan the Ape Man.

Welcome to a month rich in a variety of talents. Welcome to September.

EDGAR RICE BURROUGHS
SEPT 1, 1875-MAR 19, 1950

The man who invented the character of Tarzan was a low-paid seller of pencil sharpeners when he started reading pulp fiction. The experience of reading those stories stopped him in his tracks. "I can write stories just as rotten" he declared. Tarzan is his most famous character, and the author described this man who lived in the jungle like this: "Tarzan is a character of both immense physical strength and keen intellect."

Many actors played Tarzan, but the most famous actor is Johnny Weissmuller who perfected the Tarzan yell that summons the animals when he needs help in the jungle. Later, actress and comedian Carol Burnett would also mimic this yell for fun and to keep her voice strong.

Burroughs began to write at the age of 36, having married his sweetheart and with two children to support.

He was prolific, writing 80 novels during his greatest period of production. But he was also a war correspondent, a career that began in his sixties when the attack on Pearl Harbor occurred.

Burrough's curiosity took him to trying his hand at writing science fiction in addition to writing the Tarzan stories. His hard work paid off. Ultimately, he was considered one of the highest earners of money from his work.

Burroughs died near Tarzana, California from a heart attack at the age of 74.

Primary books by Edgar Rice Burroughs:

Tarzan of the Apes
23 Tarzan books followed

Movies that made Tarzan so popular:

Tarzan the Ape Man
Tarzan and His Mate
Tarzan Escapes

BOB NEWHART
SEPTEMBER 5, 1929-JULY 18, 2024

When comedian Bob Newhart was given a script with a joke he didn't think was funny, instead of criticizing the writer, he walked over to a dog who came to the set with his owner, got down on his knees, and read the joke to the dog. The dog never laughed.

Looking up, Newhart explained, "I knew that joke wasn't funny."

That's not the only way that Bob Newhart honed the humor that made him popular with television audiences who enjoyed sitcoms in the 20th century. But it was a way he could avoid being confrontational or complain.

Easy-going.

Newhart claimed he saw humor in the macabre. But he often delivered that darker aspect of humor in stammers and low-key mutters that made dogs and people laugh—well, people anyway.

In the beginning of his career, he was an accountant. It didn't suit him. Newhart launched a career imagining dialogues between two people and then recording them. He sent his early recordings to a record producer, and they—unlike the dog on the set later—laughed.

They signed him immediately because they thought Bob Newhart was funny.

From there he went into stand-up comedy, appearing on late night talk shows and eventually hosting *The Tonight Show* 87 times. That didn't mean he won lots of Emmy Awards. He didn't. But Newhart won television audience ratings, and fans stayed true to him.

When asked about his success, Bob theorized that, "Laughter gives us distance. It allows us to step back from an event, deal with it, and then move on."

Bob Newhart moved on for half a century or more in comedy, appearing in his later years in popular movies like *Elf, Legally Blonde 2: Red, White and Blonde,* and *Horrible Bosses.*

Married to his wife Virginia for 60 years, Newhart passed away from complications with multiple illnesses and died at the age of 94.

Television
The Bob Newhart Show
Newhart
Bob

Movies:
Elf
Horrible Bosses
Legally Blonde 2: Red, White and Blonde
On a Clear Day You Can See Forever
In & Out
Cold Turkey
Catch-22

MAURICE CHEVALIER
SEPT 12, 1888-JAN 1, 1972

Once addicted to cocaine, Maurice Chevalier said he kicked his addiction as a prisoner of war during WWI. After an uneven beginning and lots of practice Chevalier found his life's work as a performer—acting and singing.

From starring in theatrical plays to the performing his act at the Folies Bergere, Chevalier eventually came to America where he starred in two movies and was nominated for Best Actor Awards: *The Love Parade* and *The Big Pond.*

Though he doubted his own talent, Chevalier was befriended on both sides of the pond by major music makers of the day: George Gershwin, Irving Berlin, and Charlie Chaplin.

In 1932, Maurice co-starred with soprano Jeannette McDonald in *One Hour With You*, a movie that is sometimes credited with launching musicals as a preferred film medium.

Two years later, Chevalier starred in *The Merry Widow,* perhaps his best-known film today.

Later in his career, when he was cast as a wiser and seasoned Frenchman in the musical *Gigi,* Alan Jay Lerner was impressed with Chevalier's work ethic, saying that Chevalier worked harder than anyone else.

In 1958, he received an Honorary Academy Award for his contributions to entertainment.

He suffered intermittently from depression and developed kidney trouble. He died at the age of 83.

Signature Songs for Maurice Chevalier:

Valentine
Louise
Mimi
Thank Heaven for Little Girls
I Remember It Well

Popular movies:
Gigi
The Love Parade
The Big Pond

CLAUDETTE COLBERT
SEPT 13, 1903-JULY 30, 1996

French-born actress Claudette Colbert wanted to be an artist of some kind when she migrated into acting. She didn't like acting at first, but she had beauty and skills which the new form of movies—the talkies—

found valuable. She could speak both English and French.

She did just that in the movie *The Big Pond* with fellow Frenchman, Maurice Chevalier, and producers valued this linguistic skill that allowed them to film both a French and an English version of a movie, thus doubling their potential market. Claudette had a musical voice and a sophisticated bearing that was appealing to audiences.

That appeal took off when she starred opposite Clark Gable in the classic *It Happened One Night.* Despite the suggestive title, Claudette only showed a little leg during a hitchhiking scene in that movie. (Claudette showed a bit more of herself by swimming nude in a pool full of milk in the movie *The Sign of the Cross.*) Clark Gable showed more!! Taking off his shirt, he exposed his bare chest, which caused a big shift in men choosing not to wear undershirts for a while because Clark Gable, the King of Hollywood, didn't.

Social influence was beginning, and stars and movie producers were only beginning to understand the power and reach of storytelling on the screen.

Claudette won the Oscar for *It Happened One Night*, and went on to win more fans and praise in movies like *Since You Went Away* and *Tomorrow is Forever.*

At a time when other performers signed long-term contracts, Claudette didn't. She worked freelance and became one of the highest paid actresses of the 30s and 40s. As sound and color improved picture making, she retained her popularity and played opposite leading men James Stewart, Fred MacMurray, Fredric March and many others.

Married twice, Claudette Colbert lived extravagantly and well. She suffered a series of strokes that culminated in her death at the age of 92.

Movies featuring Claudette Colbert:

Arise, My Love
Since You Went Away
It Happened One Night
The Big Pond
Without Reservations
The Egg and I
Tomorrow is Forever
Parrish

AGATHA CHRISTIE
SEPT 15, 1890 — JAN 12, 1976

Agatha Christie with her daughter

The best-selling fiction writer for the ages, Queen of Mystery Agatha Christie captivated readers with her two primary characters, Hercule Poirot and Miss Jane Marple.

Both characters' prowess as detectives comes from keen powers of observation and an ability to add up what they see to find a solution to a question: Who done it? In popular parlance, that question was often written this way? *Who dunnit?*

During the Golden Age of detective stories being written, the lingo of detective stories did not infuse the writing of Agatha Christie. Rather, she explores a kind of genial hominess in her Miss Marple stories and a different brand of elitism that was not off-putting but eccentric and often very entertaining with Hercule Poirot, who often bragged that he used "his little grey cells" to figure out puzzles that others could not solve.

In addition to writing novels and short stories, Christie's work was adapted into the longest running play in theatre in the world (as of the time of this writing): *The Mousetrap.*

With fourteen collections of short stories and sixty-six novels to her credit, Agatha Christie is the most translated author in publishing history.

A British citizen, Agatha Christie was married twice. In 1926, when her first husband asked her for divorce because he had fallen in love with someone else, she disappeared. That event sparked all kinds of confusion and international headlines. Where she went and what happened to her is not known for sure, but the question itself was pursued in the movie: *Agatha*, starring Dustin Hoffman and Vanessa Redgrave.

No one knows what happened during that time. Nor did she ever explain.

When asked about herself, Christie kept her answers like this: "My chief dislikes are crowds, loud noises, gramophones and cinemas. I dislike the taste of alcohol and do not like smoking. I do like sun, sea, flowers, travelling, strange foods, sports, concerts, theatres, pianos, and doing embroidery."

Dame Agatha Christie died at the age of 85 from natural causes. Her autobiography, *Agatha Christie: An Autobiography,* was published in 1977 after her death.

Best-Selling Novels by Dame Agatha Christie:

And Then There Were None
The Murder of Roger Ackroyd
Death on the Nile
Murder on the Orient Express
A Murder is Announced

The A.B.C. Murders
Crooked House
The Pale Horse
The Mysterious Affair at Styles
Five Little Pigs
The Body in the Library
The Murder at the Vicarage

Book: *Agatha Christie: An Autobiography* by Agatha Christie

LAUREN BACALL
SEPT 16, 1924-AUG 12, 2014

Lauren Bacall's movie career was launched in the very watchable *To Have and Have Not*. She also met the man she would marry and, later, long after his death and her subsequent romances, would say Humphrey Bogart was the best husband she had ever had.

They were known as Bogart and Bacall.

Bogart was often a tough guy in movies. Bacall was a femme fatale with a look and mannerisms that others interpreted as desirable. She held her head down and looked up at you with a green/blue eyed gaze, and sometimes, she whistled. Bacall taunted Bogart in that first movie with a classic whistling dare: "You know how to whistle, don't you? You put your lips together and blow."

The chin-down move was instinctive self-preservation, Bacall confessed later. She was so nervous her chin was quivering. She lowered her chin to hide her nerves, and a femme fatale reputation was born that would always be a part of her career though as it turns out, she was a very good comedienne as well. She proved that she could deliver sharp one-liners in *How To Marry a Millionaire* and *Designing Woman.*

She played on stage, too, taking on diverse kinds of roles but one that not everyone could have tackled as she did in *Applause,* which is a reinterpretation of a classic Bette Davis movie *All About Eve*. Bette Davis gave Lauren Bacall's performance her robust approval!

Widowed when Bogart died of cancer, Bacall went on to have other romances but none as famous or intriguing as the relationship she had with Bogart.

She dallied with singer Frank Sinatra and had a sensational break-up with him. She tells that story in one of her autobiographies, *By Myself and Then Some.*

She married actor Jason Robards, but his drinking became a problem she couldn't live with. She writes about that, too.

But her relationships in real life did not eclipse her accomplishments as an actress on film, on the stage, and later in television. She is also a fine writer!

Of her career, Bacall wrote: "Stardom isn't a profession; it's an accident."

The legendary actress died of a stroke in her apartment at the age of 89.

Movies featuring Lauren Bacall:

To Have and Have Not
Key Largo
The Big Sleep
Designing Woman
Sex and the Single Girl
How to Marry a Millionaire
Written on the Wind
Bright Leaf
The Mirror Has Two Faces
Harper
Misery
The Shootist

Classic Birthdays of Popular Culture Creators of the 20th Century

Murder on the Orient Express
Appointment with Death

Books:
By Myself and Then Some by Lauren Bacall
Now by Lauren Bacall

GEORGE GERSHWIN
SEPT 26, 1898—JULY 11, 1937

By all accounts George Gershwin was a handful of creativity and joy. And that joy was translated into some of the most beautiful music in the Great American Songbook.

George's parents bought a piano for their oldest son Ira, but it was George who took to it, learned to play, and played for others as he grew up with the smiling expectation that no one wouldn't want to hear him play his piano or hear his original music.

Hyper social and generous too, Gershwin gave lavish gifts to people--like pianos to struggling and poorer composers when he could afford to buy them later in his life.

Gershwin was also a ladies' man and kept an unpublished song that he used repeatedly for wooing the ladies. "I wrote this just for you, and when I publish the song, I'll dedicate it to you."

Some women believed him.

But not everybody.

He used that same technique to make a first lunch date with a woman who understood music and men. After agreeing to meet George for lunch, she stood him up—guiltlessly, him and his lady-wooing song.

Later that same day, George saw the elusive woman at a dinner party and, disgruntled and peevish, the composer asked her, "Do you know that you stood me up for lunch?"

Smiling sweetly, this young woman who understood Gershwin's reliance upon his fame for romantic conquests replied winsomely. "Yes. I would have called you to tell you I wasn't coming, but I couldn't remember your name."

We do.

Gershwin wrote a song his daddy claimed was inspired by him just because the last line is "Come to Papa, come to Papa, do." That song is *Embraceable You,* and while Mr. Gershwin Sr. liked to request it because he thought of himself as the inspiration for it, he was wrong. *Embraceable You* was another one of George's lady-wooing songs, and he was the papa saying come to me, come to papa, do.

But George also wrote more serious music, and if you have ever seen a movie set in New York City you possibly heard a variation on the theme from *Rhapsody In Blue* that seemed to reflect the grandeur of the NYC skyline—all those skyscrapers!

We know that George Gershwin wrote *Porgy and Bess.* And he wrote a *Concerto in F.*

His last song was brought to life after his death by Ira, who was a lyric writer rather than the pianist his parents had hoped he would become. As he became better and better at matching words and syllable to musical phrases, Ira's nickname was "the jeweler" because he set a word or syllable in the framework like a jeweler places a stone in a ring.

After George's death, Ira and one of George's neglected sweethearts went through his trunk of unpublished music and helped refine and sharpen signature Gershwin songs, like *Our Love Is Here to Stay.* While the song first appeared in a movie in 1938 *The Goldwin Follies,* most people remember it best from when Gene Kelly sings it in the musical *An American in Paris.*

Five George Gershwin songs to sing:

Someone To Watch Over Me

The Man I Love

S'Wonderful

Embraceable You

I Got Rhythm

Some Sunday afternoon, treat yourself to the biopic about George Gershwin's life. It's entertaining. It's called *Rhapsody in Blue,* and it stars Robert Alda.

CATHERINE MARSHALL
SEPT 27, 1914-MARCH 18-1983

Jean Peters ably portrays Catherine Marshall, the wife in the book and movie *A Man Called Peter*

It would be difficult to overestimate how much influence Catherine Marshall had on the fabric of society in the 20th Century.

It began initially with her romantic marriage to popular preacher Peter Marshall. His untimely death led to her writing a book about her husband's life *A Man Called Peter,* and this story was made into a wonderful starring Richard Todd which inspired a generation of preachers to try and do better!

It captured the tensions preachers and their wives experience with congregations, and it also told of the young bride's personal struggle with tuberculosis.

The success of that book led to Catherine writing about her mother's work as a teacher in a series featuring a character called Christy. Television shows broadened her audience, and fans love the wholesome qualities of the books and the shows.

But that's not all.

Catherine began to write about life as a widow and her faith journey. Her second husband Leonard LeSourd, was the editor for *Guideposts* magazine, founded by Norman Vincent Peale.

Some of her most significant books include: *The Helper, Something More,* and *Beyond Ourselves.* Open and authentically honest, Marshall said this about faith and family: "I believe the old cliché, 'God helps those who help themselves,' is not only misleading but often dead wrong. My most spectacular answers to prayers have come when I was so helpless, so out of control as to be able to do nothing at all for myself."

As a writer and also an editor, Catherine Marshall was respected worldwide for her faith and her work.

She passed away at the age of 68 in 1983. She was buried beside her first husband Peter Marshall.

Movie to enjoy: *A Man Called Peter* with Richard Todd
Books to contemplate:
The Helper
Beyond Our Selves
Christy
To Live Again

ED SULLIVAN
SEPT 28, 1901-OCT 13, 1974

For twenty-three years American families spent Sunday nights in front of their still new to them televisions with Ed Sullivan and his "really big show."

The hour-long variety special introduced major talent of the century that included the Beatles, Pearl Bailey, Elvis Presley, The Jackson Five, and The Temptations.

Ed had a knack for recognizing talent. He learned it on the streets of New York chasing down stories and checking out new shows as a kind of gossip columnist—someone who kept newspaper readers up-to-date on what was happening in the entertainment field.

Though Ed was fascinated by talented people, he didn't have much stage presence himself.

When talking with guests and introducing them, Ed tucked his hands under his crossed arms to keep others from seeing his hands shaking. Because of that posture some people thought he was just stiff and called him "the wooden man."

When asked about his presence on stage, Ed said: "I've tried every way I know how to smile into a camera, but I can't do it."

The loosest Ed got on the stage was when he interviewed a continuing guest—a puppet, whom he was known to kiss. Fans loved it!

Ed Sullivan passed away at the age of 73 from cancer.

Classic Birthdays of Popular Culture Creators of the 20th Century

Good book about Ed Sullivan: *Impresario: The Life and Times of Ed Sullivan* by James Maguire

GREER GARSON
SEPT 29, 1904 — APRIL 6, 1996

Greer Garson, the woman who would one day be known as the inspiring Mrs. Miniver, began her professional career in a library as head of the research department.

Her co-worker was George Sanders, who would later become Addison DeWitt in the classic movie *All About Eve* and also play the detective in the series *The Saint*.

But at the library, it was Greer who told George that he ought to pursue a career in acting.

On the lookout for new talent, MGM producer Louis B. Mayer found Greer Garson when she was just beginning to try acting too. Mayer liked Greer Garson's looks and her voice. He signed her up for MGM, then brought her to America where he took his time finding the right role for her.

One classic movie and strong female role followed promptly, and Greer Garson made her name in *Goodbye, Mr. Chips, Pride and Prejudice, Mrs. Miniver, Random Harvest, Madame Curie, That Forsyte Woman, Valley of Decision* and *Julia Misbehaves*.

With class and a refined presence on the screen, Greer received multiple award nominations but won for Best Actress with *Mrs. Miniver.*

She was married three times, the last marriage to a man of means who supported her keen desire for philanthropy. She funded many charitable enterprises and a theatre which came with conditions, the most important being that it had a large ladies' room.

Heart trouble caused her to take up residence in a large room of her own in a Dallas hospital where she passed away at the age of 91.

Very entertaining movies featuring Greer Garson:

Goodbye Mr. Chips
Random Harvest
Mrs. Miniver
Madame Curie
Pride and Prejudice
Valley of Decision
Julia Misbehaves
That Forsyte Woman
Blossoms in the Dust

Biography: *A Rose for Mrs. Miniver: The Life of Greer Garson* by Michael Troyan

GENE AUTRY
SEPT 29, 1907-OCTOBER 2, 1998

Gene Autry was raised on the 23rd psalm.

Dirt poor and with a father who was a good provider when he felt like working, Autry said in his autobiography: "Growing up is just the price you pay to society."

That reference to prison wisdom and a kind of justice came naturally to a cowboy singer who found some of the inspiration for his songs after performing for free in prisons. Autry explained himself: "The reason so many of us would do shows in prison was because there but for the grace of God go I."

That awareness of provision from God also made Autry say as he changed jobs from working for a railroad to radio, "I was right for my time. Radio was popular. The train brought life and action to small towns."

And he knew that from experience.

Before Autry became the number one singing cowboy in the world, he was a telegraph railroad operator, receiving a visit from another famous cowboy Will Rogers. Hearing Autry strumming and singing on his guitar in the telegraph office, Rogers advised: "You ought to go to New York."

Autry didn't go right away. He was drawing a good wage with the telegraph office and sending home money to his mama.

He decided to check out the possibilities in New York before quitting his job.

Autry took a train to New York and auditioned for work. People there told him he needed practice singing in front of people. They advised him to, "Stick with yodeling."

Autry yodeled and sang and rode a horse and in his startling way became associated with a form of the musical western called the Horse Opera. That is, he was a singing cowboy the way Roy Rogers and Dale Evans would be, too.

But for Autry, singing was just a way of keeping others company and telling stories. Autry became famous for making popular four non-religious and now very popular Christmas songs: *Rudolph the Red-Nosed Reindeer, Frosty the Snowman, Up on the Housetop,* and *Here Comes Santa Claus.*

But he is also associated with a song many mothers sang to babies when they rocked them. "You are my sunshine. My only sunshine. You make me happy when skies are grey."

While famous as the Singing Cowboy, Autry also had some strong beliefs about what makes a good cowboy, and even he admits that his values are akin to being a grown-up Boy Scout. But here are Autry's rules for handling yourself right as a cowboy:

The Cowboy must never shoot first, hit a smaller man, or take unfair advantage.

He must never go back on his word or a trust confided in him.

He must always tell the truth.

He must be gentle with children, the elderly, and animals.

He must not advocate or possess racially or religiously intolerant ideas.

He must help people in distress.

He must be a good worker.

He must keep himself clean in thought, speech, action, and personal habits.

He must respect women, parents, and his nation's laws.

The Cowboy is a patriot.

Gene Autry died at the age of 91 of lymphoma.

Signature Songs
Tumbling Tumbleweeds, Frosty the Snowman, Here Comes Santa Claus, Rudolph the Red-nosed Reindeer

Five movies featuring Gene Autry:

Comin' Round the Mountain
The Singing Cowboy

Classic Birthdays of Popular Culture Creators of the 20th Century

Tumbling Tumbleweeds
Melody Ranch
The Singing Hill
Back in the Saddle

JOHNNY MATHIS
SEPTEMBER 30, 1935 —

While Johnny Mathis might have become an accomplished athlete (high-jumper), he took his daddy's advice and pursued a career in music instead.

It was a good choice. The young man from Gilmer, Texas got his start at age 19, and his career is still going strong in 2025. "I have no memories of my childhood in Texas. When I was about four, we moved to San Francisco. I was in the middle of seven brothers and sisters: three girls and four boys. Most of my older brothers and sisters got the blame for everything, and the little ones had a free ride. We loved each other but fought like cats and dogs."

"Dad would come home from doing odd jobs.... and then we'd play that piano. I'll be eternally grateful to him."

Johnny Mathis can sing any kind of music. People who grew up with him have a broad choice of possible favorites from the American standard songbook which Mathis made popular:

A Certain Smile
What Will My Mary Say?
Too Much, Too Little, Too Late
When a Child Is Born
Maria
The Twelfth of Never
Chances Are
Wild Is the Wind
Where Do I Begin?
You're All I Need to Get By

Mathis says of his ongoing and very long career as a popular music singer: "I've never been married, and I have no regrets about not starting my own family. I come from a large one, so there are so many people around all the time. I've been happy. That's about the size of it. I would have been a good father because I've been a father to my brothers' and sisters' children."

Johnny Mathis is still going strong, drawing crowds of fans all over the country who enjoy the classics which he helped to make popular.

DEBORAH KERR
SEPT 30, 1921-OCT 16, 2007

"I respect anyone who has to fight and howl for his decency," said Deborah Kerr, a Scottish-born actress who trained for six months to get rid of her accent.

Speaking American English won Kerr more parts, but her ladylike refinement was part of her allure. You see her dressed down in *The Sundowners* and *Separate Tables*, but underneath her less glamourous roles she still embodies that essence of mature character.

She was always a lady—often, a well-bred, well-dressed lady. Her sensibilities, refined and tasteful, often drew the attention of many on-screen male heroes.

Clark Gable found her irresistible in *The Hucksters*.

Yul Brenner danced with her in *The King and I*.

Cary Grant waited for her at the top of the Empire State Building in *An Affair to Remember.*

And Burt Lancaster splashed on the beach with her in *From Here to Eternity.*

She flirted with Robert Mitchum in *The Grass is Greener,* worked with him in *The Sundowners,* and was his war ally in *Heaven Knows, Mr. Allison.*

Although nominated six times for an Oscar for Best Actress, she did not win; but in 1994, the Academy awarded her an Honorary Oscar for her body of work.

A very popular actress without much scandal or politics to attach to her name, Deborah Kerr withdrew from acting in the 60's because she was repulsed by the explicit sex and bad language. She retired to Switzerland and Spain.

Living quietly, she developed Parkinson's and died at the age of 86.

Classic Birthdays of Popular Culture Creators of the 20th Century

Popular Movies with Deborah Kerr:

From Here to Eternity

Separate Tables

An Affair to Remember

The Prisoner of Zenda

The King and I

King Solomon's Mines

The Hucksters

The Grass is Greener

Heaven Knows, Mr. Allison

The Sundowners

EXCERPT FROM BLESSED:STORIES CONFESSIONS OF A RECOVERING CAREGIVER

Since my three-year stint as my father's caregiver, I wrestle with socially unacceptable urges to comfort, feed, and water just about anybody.

I do not have to know you personally to offer you a cough drop when you choke. I say "Bless you" before you finish sneezing, and my right hand will automatically fidget for an Aloe-enriched, bacteria-killing tissue.

After your third sneeze, I will tell you the names of cold products you need although these medicines are not only what I think promote healing. Sick people need to go to bed and rest and drink plenty of fluids and be waited on by people like me.

I am ready to do that. I am a recovering caregiver always on the lookout for someone who needs a caregiver—that is me. And I know that my attentions mostly wear on people's nerves.

My teenage niece Katie is tired of hearing me say, "Button up. Buckle up. Wash your hands."

Sometimes I tire of hearing myself, but I cannot stop. It is cold outside, accidents do happen, and illness-bearing germs should be washed away.

This type of other-oriented watchful vigilance is not confined only to matters of wellness.

Recently stuck in a bad traffic jam on the interstate, I opened my car trunk where I store some caregiving supplies and walked up and down the steaming asphalt giving away free bottles of water to other stuck drivers. It was a very satisfying experience—so many thirsty people, and me with so much water to share.

That caregiver urge!—I overflow with it.

On an idling airport shuttle bus the other day, the driver asked the already seated passengers if we would be responsible to not let another person get on if he left the doors open so we could have fresh air while we watched.

Other passengers nodded politely.

I got excited, for no one believes in the benefits of fresh air more than a recovering caregiver.

I watched hard. Two people got on. I asked the lady beside me, "What are we supposed to do now?"

"It's not our job to guard that door," she said, shrugging.

My jaw dropped. I was envious of that shrug, for I have lost track of the boundaries of socially acceptable helpfulness, and I know it. I am labeled by others as codependent, hypervigilant, and addicted--one of those suckers born every minute.

But I wasn't born in a minute. My condition evolved over time while I handled medical emergencies for a dying man and forgot who I was, except as a caregiver. I have emerged from that experience in hyper-helpful mode. I watch. I warn. I offer. I am a recovering caregiver, and there's no twelve-step program to rehabilitate me.

But you could. And you could help others like me or who may become like me. First, you have to see caregivers. They live and move among you, but they are very adept at being invisible.

To find one, simply look beside a person suffering from age-related disorders or a debilitating disease. Beside a chronic patient is a barely alive, almost invisible caregiver. *See that caregiver*? Speak to him. To her. Speak these words slowly: "How are you?"

If she replies, "Fine," smile reassuringly. Send fresh fruit to her house anyway. Or send a fresh flower. Drop off fresh milk. Fresh bread. Her life is mostly stale, and she can't easily drive to a store for fresh stuff. You get the idea.

Does it seem like a small idea and, therefore, unnecessary? Think again.

Any gesture or gift of care for a current caregiver who has forgotten her own needs will become a potent memory that will surface later like medicine from a dissolving gel capsule that releases a healing dose of self-recognition and the restorative message: It's okay to accept help rather than only give it.

But don't over-react. If a recovering caregiver you know is already loose and roaming around compulsively offering Band-aids, water, cough drops, and tissues, don't resist her. Instead, simply accept everything a former caregiver offers, and say, "Thank you!" Caregivers haven't heard those words in ages.

Rather than feed an addiction for approval, which some experts warn is what makes caregivers who they are, that expression of simple courtesy will help a caregiver exhale and finally say to someone, "You're so very welcome."

The job is done then. See? She is finished. He can let go. Say good-bye.

I know.

Every time I say those words, I say good-bye to my old caregiver self and breathe hello to the people who live in the world where I can imagine being on a shuttle bus sitting near a just-about-to-sneeze, almost-gonna-cough, possibly thirsty person, and--oh, bliss--simply shrug.

BOOKS BY DAPHNE SIMPKINS

Non-fiction books about caregiving:

Classic Birthdays of 20th Century Popular Culture Creators Book 1 January-March

Classic Birthdays of 20th Century Popular Culture Creators Book 2 April-June

Classic Birthdays of 20th Century Popular Culture Creators Book 3 July-September

Classic Birthdays of 20th Century Popular Culture Creators Book 4 October – December (coming soon!)

11 DIY Holiday Talks   Book 5

The Long Good Night, a memoir

What Al Left Behind: Stories about Caregiving Book 1

Blessed: Stories about Caregiving Book 2

Fiction with a caregiving theme:

Belle: A Mildred Budge Friendship Story

Lovejoy: a novel about desire

Tricks of the Mind

The Mildred Budge novels:

Mildred Budge in Cloverdale book 1
Mildred Budge in Embankment book 2
The Bride's Room book 3
Kingdom Come book 4

The Short Adventures of Mildred Budge:

Miss Budge in Love book 1
The Mission of Mildred Budge book 2
Miss Budge Goes to Fountain City book 3

Stand-Alone Fiction

Christmas in Fountain City

Essays and Memoirs

A Cookbook for Katie
What Makes a Man a Hero?

ABOUT Daphne Simpkins

Daphne Simpkins is best known for her series featuring retired schoolteacher Mildred Budge and her church going friends. However, she writes extensively on caregiving and other matters about daily life. To keep up with new releases, follow her on Amazon, Facebook, and Goodreads.

www.ingramcontent.com/pod-product-compliance
Lightning Source LLC
Chambersburg PA
CBHW071954070426
42453CB00008BA/667

"The call to give is often met with tension in today's church. But with the mind of a theologian and the heart of a shepherd, Dr. Swartz carefully tackles a sensitive subject with grace, compassion, and clarity, guiding the reader to a better understanding of the heart of God. In a biblically compelling argument, he explains not only how Christians are to give but why we are to do so. This book includes practical teaching on giving, but even more, provides a pathway to a life of real joy focused on worshiping the Lord with a generous heart. It will awaken within you a greater willingness to give to the Lord's work and a more profound joy in doing so. After reading Joyful Generosity: Responding to God's Grace, I have a greater desire to give to Kingdom work, a clearer view of God's heart, and a more intense longing for heaven."

– *Dr. Michael Staton, Senior Pastor of First Baptist Church of Mustang, Oklahoma, and featured speaker of Every Word Preached, www.everywordpreached.com.*

"Joyful Generosity: Responding to God's Grace is a spiritually powerful, biblical-theological approach to the subject of financial stewardship. Dr. Swartz takes the reader from Genesis to Revelation to build a compelling case for generous giving to the local church. His approach is balanced: he avoids the heresies of prosperity theology while teaching God's clear commands and promises related to giving. I especially appreciated his unique biblical arguments for the validity and importance of a dedicated physical space in which to worship God and study His word. I highly recommend this book to anyone wanting a God-centered and audience-sensitive exposition of biblical giving. I will be providing this book to the pastors in all our capital campaigns."

– *Dr. Rod Rogers, Owner/principal consultant with AMI Church Consulting Services, www.abundantgiving.com.*